Contents

1. Introduction

2. The Main Players

3. So Why Did the Battle Take Place?

4. The Build-up to the Battle

5. Let Battle Commence!

6. Aftermath of the Battle and the Return of Percy!

Questionnaire Survey

Photographs

Bibliography

Acknowledgements
I am very grateful to Mr Les Hall (Curator and Guide at Battlefield Church), Mr Frank Bailey (Chairman of Trustees, Battlefield) and Mr M. Connor (my History teacher at Kingsland Grange School) for all their help and encouragement in writing this book, and to Mrs Ruth Othen at Livesey Limited for helping to put it all together and print it.

The Battle of Shrewsbury
Saturday, 21st July, 1403

1. Introduction

Did you know, that nearly 600 years ago, an amazing battle took place right on your doorstep in the fields of Shrewsbury? It's true!

A battle called by those at the time:
"we shall scarcely find any battle in those ages where the shock was more terrible" (Ref. 8).

And again:
"never saw . . . so furious a battle in so short a time (2-3 hours) or of larger casualties than happened here" (Ref. 8).

This was a battle which could have changed the history of England . . . but didn't.

The battlefield is only 4 kms from my house. You can go and see it yourself if you like. And as you stand there in the fields, you can imagine what it was like on that Saturday afternoon, 21st July, 1403, when 6,000 men were killed!

Have I whetted your appetite? . . . Then let me tell you the true story of the Battle of Shrewsbury . . .

Saturday, 21st July, 1403

SIR HENRY PERCY's SIDE

Thomas, Earl of Worcester

Henry, Earl of Northumberland
Not present at the battle

———— BROTHERS ————

SIR HENRY PERCY
'Hotspur' – eldest son of the Earl of Northumberland

Earl of Douglas (Scottish)
Sir Richard Venables
Sir Richard Vernon
Owain Glyndwr – never turned up!

KING HENRY IV's SIDE

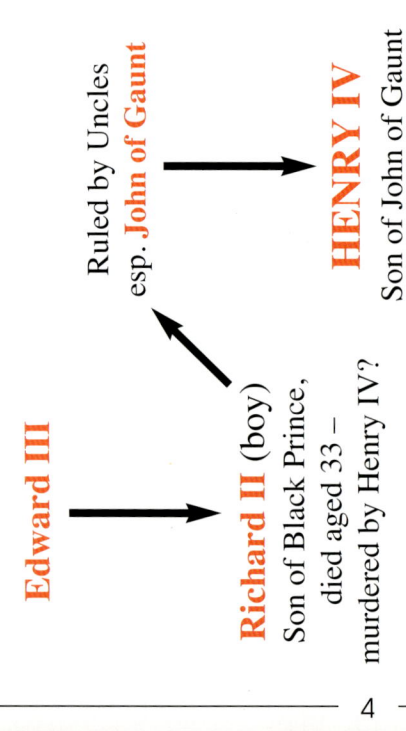

Edward III

Richard II (boy)
Son of Black Prince, died aged 33 – murdered by Henry IV?

Ruled by Uncles esp. **John of Gaunt**

HENRY IV
Son of John of Gaunt

Prince of Wales
15-year-old son of Henry IV and later to become Henry V

Earl of Stafford and Earl of Dunbar

2. The Main Players

Firstly, let's look at the main players in the battle.

The Battle of Shrewsbury was between:

Henry IV.v.Sir Henry Percy

Henry IV was the King of England. On his side, he had Henry, his son (who later became Henry V) – at the moment, though, he was just the Prince of Wales, and, at the time of the battle, he was only 15 years old. Could you go in to battle aged only 15? Also on Henry IV's side, he had the **Earl of Stafford** and the **Earl of Dunbar**.

Sir Henry Percy (his nickname was 'Hotspur', because he was so hot-tempered and impetuous! and he was also sometimes called 'Harry') had on his side, his Uncle, the **Earl of Worcester**, the **Earl of Douglas** (who was Scottish), **Sir Richard Venables** and **Sir Richard Vernon**.

Percy's father, the Early of Northumberland was too ill to fight with his son, and was later pardoned by Henry IV.

Percy was planning to join up with the Welsh chieftain, **Owain Glyndwr**, who also hated the English king, but Owain Glyndwr never turned up!

King Henry IV

3. So Why Did the Battle Take Place?

Well, the simple answer is that Percy was really mad with Henry IV and wanted to take over as king himself. You see, in the late 1300s, the King of England was **Edward III**. When he died, **Richard II** became King. But Richard was only a boy and so the country was ruled by his uncles, one of whom was **John of Gaunt**. John of Gaunt's son was Henry (the Henry IV we're talking about).

Now, Henry had a quarrel with Richard II and Richard banished Henry out of the country for six years! He also took all Henry's estates (land and buildings). So, as you can imagine, Henry was also mad at Richard II. So one day, Henry took his revenge! He secretly sailed back, across the North Sea, and landed in Yorkshire. There, he gathered together many supporters, who also disliked Richard. He locked Richard up and took the throne for himself – he became King Henry IV.

Richard was held prisoner at Pontefract Castle where he is said to have been starved to death in 1400, at the age of 33. All his life, Henry regretted the terrible way he had treated Richard.

So the country was split between those who supported Henry, and those who resented him for what he had done to Richard, whom they had supported.

Percy was a Richard supporter and did not want Henry as King, even though, at one time, they had been friends. He blamed Henry for the death of Richard II and said Henry had broken his oath that he *'would ever remain faithful to Richard'* (Ref. 8).

But Percy also had other reasons to hate King Henry. You see, for years, Percy had been patrolling the border with Scotland to keep the Scots out (the Scots were always trying to invade England). He did a great job, but Henry refused to pay his expenses or properly reward him. Then, one day, Percy captured a very important Scotsman – the Earl of Douglas. He expected Henry to reward him handsomely for this, but Henry refused (he said he had no money left after fighting the Welsh!) So Percy refused to hand over the Earl of Douglas and this increased the enmity between him and the King. And that's not the end of it!

Percy was also fed up with King Henry because, after two years, Henry had still not done anything to get Percy's friend, Roger Mortimer, released from being held captive by Owain Glyndwr.

Henry had also put up taxes, despite his promise not to. **So to Percy, Henry was a man who lied and broke his promises** and the *'impatient spirit of Percy'* *'sought to overthrow the precarious title of Henry.'* (Ref. 8).

So, for all these reasons, Percy wanted to put an end to King Henry IV . . .

Drawn by my friend, Rupert Parry

4. The Build-up to the Battle

Sir Henry Percy ('Hotspur') was up in Northumberland, on the Scottish border. In early July, 1403, he marched south with 200 men, intent on revolting against the King. His old enemy, the Earl of Douglas (whom, you will remember, he had captured) joined him, more than happy to have a chance to fight the English King! Percy also had with him, his uncle, the Earl of Worcester.

Percy raised most of his bowmen from the people of Cheshire. He persuaded them by saying that Richard II was still alive! (remember, they didn't have newspapers or TV in those days so, often, people didn't know the news). Cheshire and Chester were later heavily fined for having supported Percy. In fact, they thought they were fighting for Richard II (who was, by then, dead!) and they went into battle wearing Richard's emblem – a hart (a deer).

Percy then marched on Shrewsbury, where he had arranged to meet up with the Welsh chieftain, Owain Glyndwr (who was also happy to have the chance of fighting King Henry). But, Owain Glyndwr never turned up!

Meanwhile, King Henry was over in Nottingham, on his way to support Percy against the Scots! When he heard that Percy was raising an army against him, he raced west towards Shrewsbury, gathering more forces on the way. Henry's son, Prince Henry, the Prince of Wales (later to become Henry V) was, already, at the age of 15, commanding a small garrison at Shrewsbury. Shrewsbury's citizens were loyal to King Henry and hated the Welsh, who were always attacking Shropshire towns and villages.

The King got to Shrewsbury first and took command of Shrewsbury Castle. On seeing this, Percy drew back and took up position at Berwick, just north of the town. You can imagine his dismay when he remembered that it had been foretold to him, years earlier, that he would die at Berwick! (he thought it meant the town of Berwick, which is on the Scottish border!) He became even more worried when, on the morning of the battle, he discovered that he'd left his sword at Berwick – not a good start!

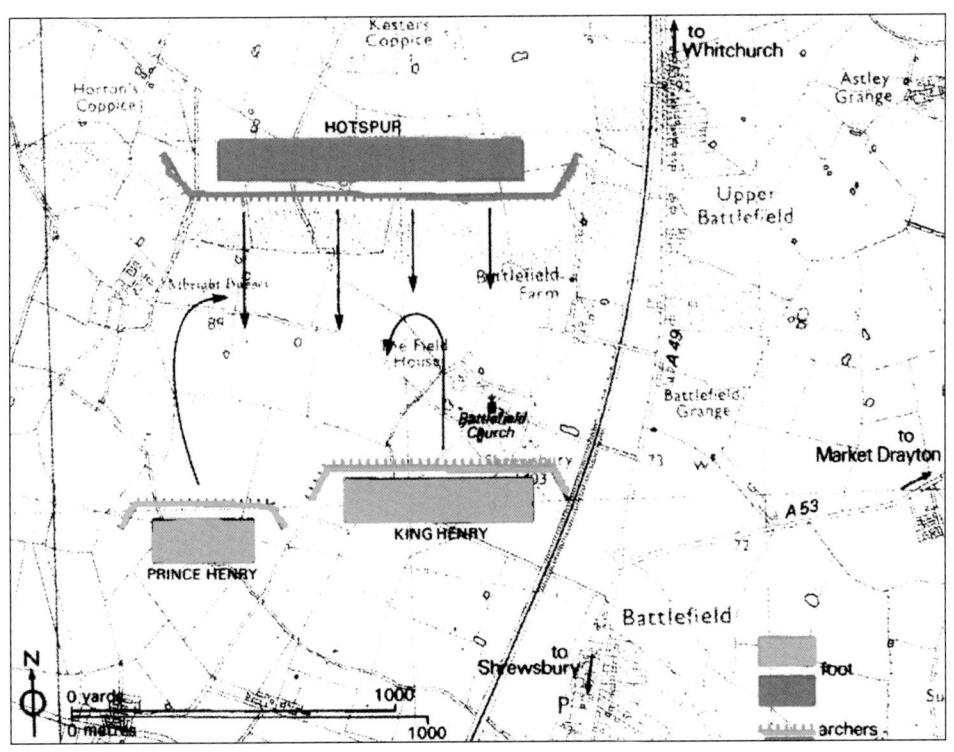

The site of the Battle of Shrewsbury.

5. Let Battle Commence!

It's Saturday, 21st July, 1403 and everyone is very nervous! King Henry has the larger army – about 12,000 men compared to Percy's 10,000 men. Imagine it, 22,000 men marching out on that morning to face each other, armed with the famous English longbow, crossbows, swords, lances, spears, bills and daggers! – wouldn't you be nervous? Some had horses, but most were foot-soldiers ('Men-at-Arms'). You can see what they looked like and what they wore on the inside front cover and page 3.

The exact site of the battlefield is uncertain, but the Royal Charter for the church says it was built on the site of the battlefield. There are some photographs of the battlefield and the church on pages 13-16.

Percy stationed his army on the higher ground behind a field of peas and ordered his men to plait the peas together to impede the King – but it didn't do much good.

On the morning of 21st July, King Henry marched north out of Shrewsbury to confront Percy at Harlescott. The two great armies faced each other (about 600 metres apart – out of range) for several hours, while the King tried to negotiate. Percy had sent the King a manifesto listing his complaints. Eventually, two hours before sunset, the negotiations broke down. Percy tried to delay, hoping that Owain Glyndwr would arrive, but the King knew this and wanted to get on with it before nightfall.

So the order was given and the trumpet sounded and, with their hearts in their mouths, the two armies marched towards each other.

For the first time in history, it was English longbow against English longbow. Both sides had a large number of archers – that's why so many were killed in the battle.

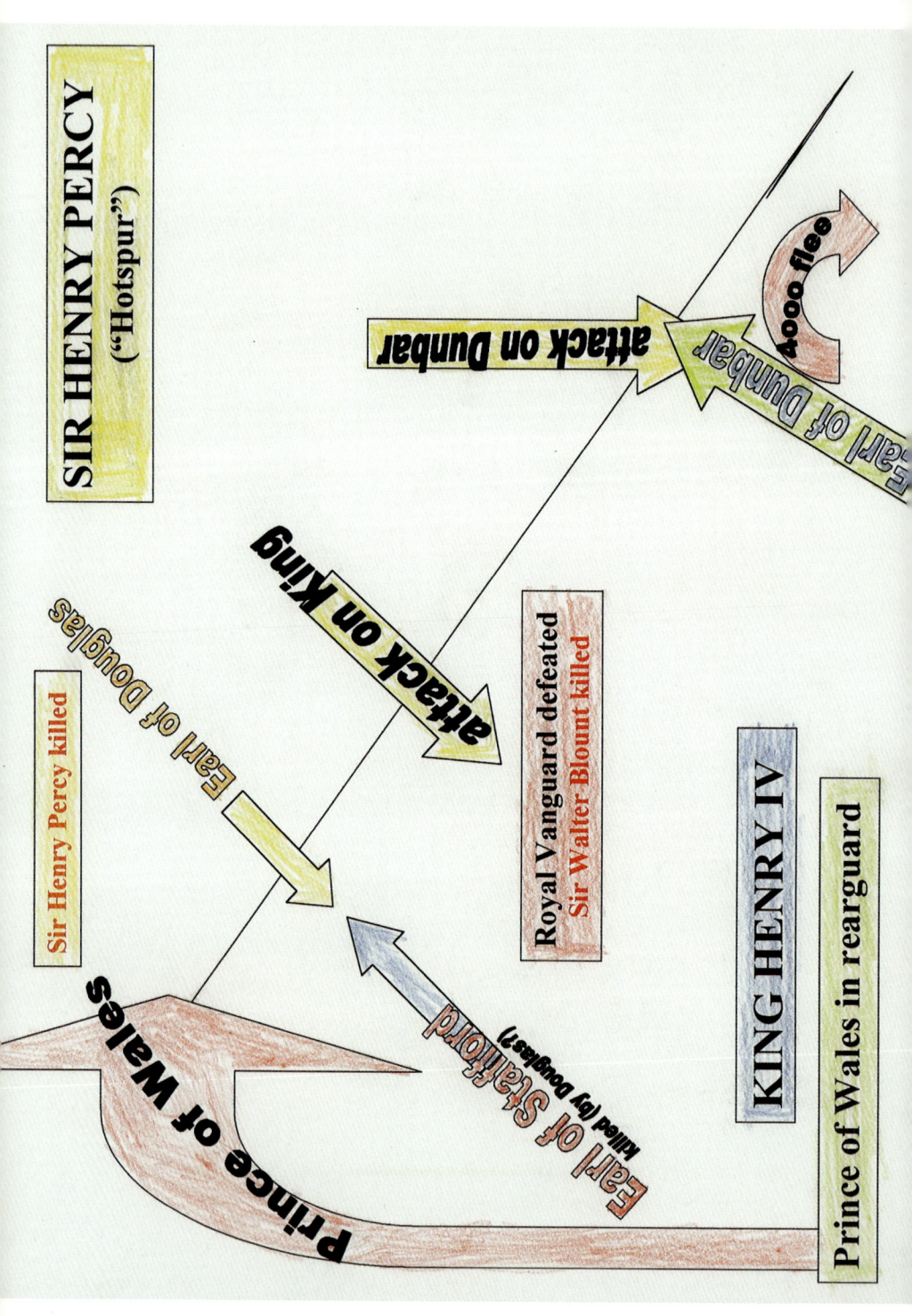

The battlefield site today

The higher ground where Sir Henry Percy ('Hotspur') probably took up position.

The so-called 'Field of Arrows', next to the present-day church.

The battlefield site today

Probably the 'Field of Peas', where 'Hotspur' tried to hamper the advance of Henry IV's troops by weaving together the pea plants.

The lawn, shown here, is thought to be the burial pit, or trench, where some 1,600 men (and horses) were buried after the battle. Many bones were found in the 1800s.

The Church of St Mary Magdalene at Battlefield.

'Substantially unchanged after nearly 600 years, the church stands in solitary splendour amongst the quiet fields of rural Shropshire, marking the burial place of many hundreds who fell in an exceptionally hard fought fight.'

The church is so called because the Battle of Shrewsbury was fought on the eve of the Feast of St Mary Magdalene (21st July). The church was established by Royal Charter of Henry IV to offer prayers for those killed. An effigy of King Henry IV can be seen on its east front (see page 16).

ST. MARY MAGDALENE, BATTLEFIELD.

THIS CHURCH IS MAINTAINED BY THE REDUNDANT CHURCHES FUND, WITH MONEY PROVIDED BY PARLIAMENT AND THE CHURCH OF ENGLAND, AND BY THE GIFTS OF THE PUBLIC. ALTHOUGH NO LONGER USED FOR REGULAR WORSHIP, IT REMAINS A CONSECRATED BUILDING.

The Church of St Mary Magdalene at Battlefield showing the East Front with the effigy of King Henry IV.

Signs and street names in the vicinity of the battlefield.

The model of the Battle of Shrewsbury that I made with my dad (each figure represents 200 men).

A detail from the model showing the death of Sir Walter Blount, Royal Standard Bearer to King Henry IV.

The archers were in front, with the Men-at-Arms behind. Remember, King Henry had the most men (12,000), compared to Percy's 10,000, but Percy had the advantage of the higher ground.

The King's Vanguard, led by the Earl of Stafford, moved forward and unleashed a *'thick cloud of arrows'*. Percy cried *'Sound off all the instruments of war'* (Henry IV – Part I) and his archers opened fire aiming at the Royal Vanguard and the Earl of Dunbar, who *'fell like apples fallen in the Autumn'*. At this, 4,000 of the King's men fled!

When most of the arrows were exhausted, hand to hand fighting began. Percy, the Earl of Douglas and about 30 men launched a personal attack on the King:

'Percy performed feats of valour which are almost incredible; he seemed determined that the King of England should, that day, fall by his arm. He sought him all over the field of battle'. (Ref. 8).

And, he nearly succeeded:

'Henry exposed his person in the thickest of the fight'.

They charged the Royal Standard to hack their way through to the King.

But Henry had two or three decoys, dressed as himself, to confuse Percy! One of these was Sir Walter Blount, the King's Royal Standard Bearer. In the attack on the King, Sir Walter Blount was killed, and the Earl of Stafford was also killed (by Douglas?).

The Royal army counter-attacked. The Prince of Wales (aged only 15), advanced on the left and was wounded with an arrow gash to his face (a scar he carried with him for the rest of his life). The Prince pressed inwards, attacking Percy's line on the left flank and rear. In the savage mêlée that followed, Sir Henry Percy was killed, possibly by an arrow in the face when he momentarily lifted his visor.

When the King's decoys were killed, Percy's side thought they had killed the King and shouted *'all's done, all's won!'* and *'Henry Percy, King!'* The King replied *'Henry Percy is dead!'* . . . as indeed he was. When they heard this, Percy's army fled the battlefield and were pursued by the King's men over a 3-mile rout. Many of them were killed, wounded or captured. The Earl of Douglas was chased to Haughmond Hill where, after falling and breaking his leg, he was captured. Also captured were the Earl of Worcester, Sir Richard Venables and Sir Richard Vernon.

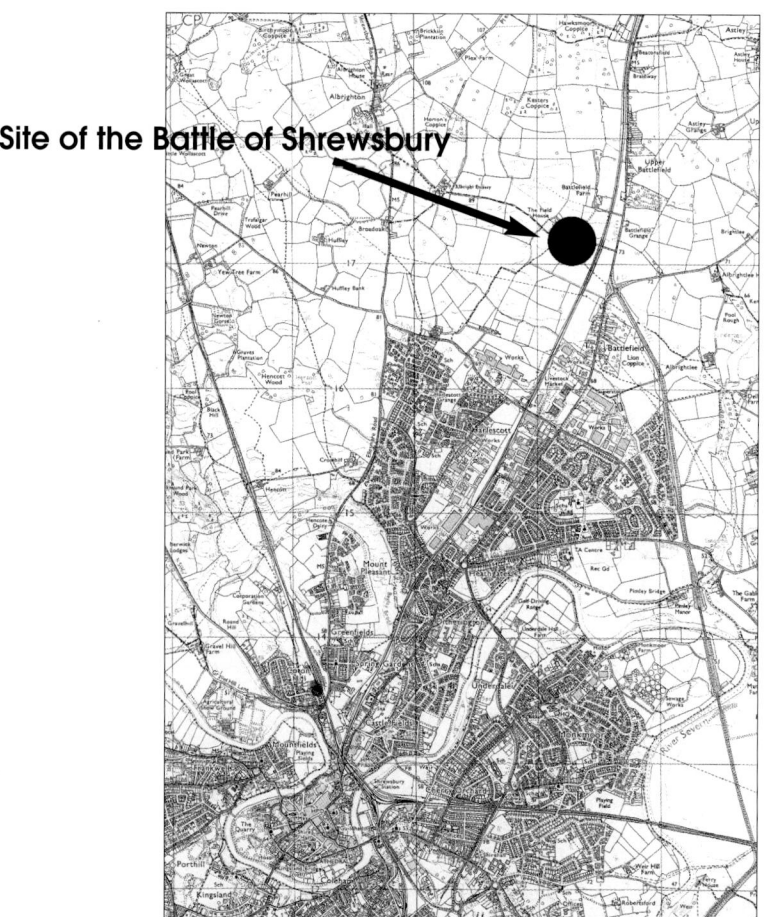

Site of the Battle of Shrewsbury

6. Aftermath of the Battle

In 2-3 short hours, and just before dark, 6,000 men lay dead (27.27% of the total number who fought) and 3,000-4,000 were wounded. Many died later of their wounds. A temporary field hospital was set up near the battlefield with feather-beds for the wounded – this is where Featherbed Lane, Harlescott now is and from where it got its name (see photograph on the inside back cover).

There were an exceptional number of dead and wounded and there were particularly heavy losses on the King's side. The King lost 16-28 Royal Knights on that day and 8 of Percy's knights were killed.

Sixteen hundred men and horses were buried in a large pit or trench on the battlefield. This is where the Battlefield Church now stands (see photographs). Many bones were found here in the 1800s. Other burials took place over a 3-mile radius of the battlefield.

The dead and wounded lay on the battlefield and, as the sun was setting, their bodies were looted and stripped.

King Henry IV was thought to be the most valiant knight that day, killing 30-36 men (in effect, he won the 'Man of the Match' award!) Percy, too, was described as *'a renowned and noble lord'* and *'the flower and glory of Christian knighthood.'* The King and the captured Earl of Worcester wept over Percy's dead body, but, whatever the King's personal feelings for his one-time friend, Percy and his supporters were guilty of High Treason and they had to be made an example of – justice had to be seen to be done!

Owain Glyndwr never crossed the River Severn that day, and, after the battle, he went back to Wales – the Rebellion was over!

Initially, Percy was buried at Whitchurch. Then the King ordered that his body be dug up and put on display. They did that in those days to prove that someone was really dead. Percy's body was displayed in Shrewsbury (at the top of Pride Hill) between two millstones. His body was then drawn and quartered and the parts displayed in public in Newcastle, London, Chester and Bristol. His head was displayed in York. Just before Christmas, 1403 his remains were returned to his widow and buried (see next page).

Regarding the others captured, the King ordered that no-one was to leave the country. Worcester, Venables and Vernon were tried for treason on Monday, 23rd July, 1403. Worcester refused to ask for the King's mercy. They were all hanged in Shrewsbury Castle that very day and then drawn and quartered – and all only two days after the battle.

Worcester's head was displayed on London Bridge until, in December, it was buried with his body in Shrewsbury Abbey. The heads of Venables and Vernon were displayed in Chester as a warning to those who might think of trying the same thing.

Some rebels were pardoned. A general pardon was given to all Percy's supporters who, four months and one day after the battle, asked for pardon. Because the Earl of Douglas was Scottish, he was not executed, but he was held prisoner. The King's supporters were rewarded with the proceeds from Percy's estates. The knight who captured the Earl of Douglas was given 100 Marks a year!

And that is the end of the story of the Battle of Shrewsbury – isn't it a fantastic episode in our rich history of England?

The Return of Percy

One day in December, 1403, Lady Percy had a knock on the door, it was the Postman. The Postman had a parcel for her.

She said: 'Oh is it for me? It must be from my Aunt Maud for Christmas.'

At once she tore off the paper: 'Aaaaaaar!' she cried, 'it's Harry and he's in bits . . . and a bit whiffy!'

'Oh Harry, do pull yourself together!' she said.

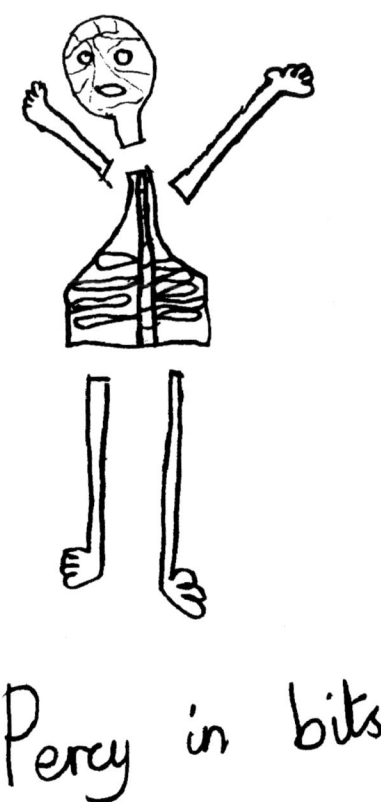

Percy in bits

Questionnaire Survey

Having learnt all about the Battle of Shrewsbury, I wondered how much local people know of this famous battle. So I decided to do a Questionnaire Survey to find out. The results show that whilst most local people had heard of the battle, not many knew much more about it – like who took part; who won; why did it take place in Shrewsbury; where is the battlefield site?

I know it happened nearly 600 years ago, but it was a very famous battle and it happened right here in Shrewsbury.

Luckily, more is now being made of the battlefield site and a Battle of Shrewsbury Heritage Site is being provided at the site to tell the story of this famous battle. And there are still local placenames that reflect the battle – some of the photographs show these.

The year 2003 will be the 600th anniversary of the battle. A big celebration took place in July 1903 to mark the 500th anniversary. I wonder if anything will be done to mark the 600th anniversary – I hope so!

It was tough if you were on the losing side! This plaque can be seen at the top of Pride Hill (on the wall of Barclays Bank). See 'Aftermath of the Battle', on page 21.

Inside Battlefield Church today. Most of the church was built by 1409 (apart from the tower, which was added about a century later). No trace of the college buildings, attached to the church, remain today above ground. The photograph just shows (in the roof), the coats of arms of some of those who fought in the battle. These were put there in 1861.

Hello. I am doing a History project on the Battle of Shrewsbury and I'm trying to find out how much people know about the Battle. I'm doing a Questionnaire Survey & I wonder if you would mind answering a few questions.

Battle of Shrewsbury

QUESTIONNAIRE

Number

1. Have you heard of the Battle of Shrewsbury?

2. How do you know about it?

3. In what year, or what Century, did it take place?

4. Can you show me on this map where it took place?

5. Who was the Battle between?

6. Who won?

7. Do you know why it took place?

8. Why did it take place in Shrewsbury?

9. Do you think the Battle & the Battle site should have more/less/the same publicity?

10. Do you think people would be interested/not interested in visiting the Battle site and learning more about it?

Do you want to say anything else?

Thank you very much

Bibliography
(where I found my information)

1. **'The Battle of Shrewsbury 1403'**
   by E. J. Priestly – 1979

2. **'Shrewsbury and Shropshire' (Chapter 6)**
   by Dorothy P. H. Wrenn – 1968

3. **'Henry IV – Part I':** BBC Video

4. **Mr Les Hall**
   (Curator and Guide at Battlefield Church) on 9th May, 1999 and many subsequent visits

5. **Encarta '96 Encyclopedia**
   CD Rom – 1996

6. **The Hutchinson History Library**
   CD Rom – 1996

7. **'Battlefields of Britain'**
   by David Smurthwaite – 1984

8. **'The History of England'**
   by David Hume – 1831

Published by Hugh Kent, Shrewsbury © 2000
Tel: 01743 359241. E-mail: hugh.kent@lineone.net
Illustrations by Dominic Kent
ISBN: 0-9539784-0-0